The Dedalus Press

Poems for Breakfast

Enda Wyley

Also by Enda Wyley from The Dedalus Press

"Eating Baby Jesus"

"Socrates in the Garden"

POEMS FOR BREAKFAST

ENDA WYLEY

The Dedalus Press
24 The Heath ~ Cypress Downs ~ Dublin 6W
Ireland

Cover Painting: "Breakfast Bowl" by Sarah Kernaghan
Cover design by Gavin Beattie

ISBN 1 904556 19 1 (paper)
ISBN 1 904556 20 5 (bound)

Acknowledgements are due to *Poetry Ireland Review*, *The Irish Times*, *The Independent* (London), *Poetry Review*, *A Conversation Piece*, *Poetry and Art*, The National Museums and Galleries of Northern Ireland and Abbey Press, *Irish Writers Against the War*, O'Brien Press, Lyric Fm, Ropes, *Southward*, *De Braake Hond* (Belgium), The Stinging Fly, *New Hibernia Review* (U.S.A.) The *Out to Lunch* Series, Bank of Ireland, *The Enchanted Way*, RTE Radio 1, *Forgotten Light*, *Memory Poems*, A. & A. Farmar. Special thanks also to my parents Jack and Imelda and to my brothers and sisters, Shay, Róisín, Alan and Dervla.

Dedalus Press books are represented and distributed in the U.S.A. and Canada by **Dufour Editions Ltd.**, P.O. Box 7, Chester Springs, Pennsylvania 19425
in the UK by **Central Books**, 99 Wallis Road, London E9 5LN

The Dedalus Press receives financial assistance from
An Chomhairle Ealaíon, The Arts Council, Ireland.
Printed in Dublin by Johnswood Press

For
Peter Sirr

CONTENTS

DISH OF A MOON
For Martin Drury

'But then it's the light / that makes you remember.'
Yehuda Amichai, *Forgetting Someone*.

He gets up to pace the house late at night —
is an anxious adult shutting doors, winding the clock,
pulling out plugs, making the dripping tap stop:
but on the landing he looks out to check the light,

neighbours' roof-tops, his trees, the weather.
Wind tugs at the moon that is a memory
wide and yellow and he is a tide of worry
dragged back again to what he will never forget — his mother

kneeling beside him, her eight year old child, mopping
his night-time sweats away with her sweet made-up tune.
Lady moon, Lady moon, she sings to the high dish of a moon —
nearly forty years on, he swears he can still hear her singing

and feel her arms tight around him, her finger
pointing down to two foxes who have found their way
into the garden through the wood of time. Their eyes up say
The moon is a light left on — its light there to make you remember.

Two Women in Kosovo

'I'm going to jump,' her sister whispers,
holding out her hand.
And so they jump together — so naturally
they might be young girls again
leaping at waves on their holidays, jumping
across rivers on their way to school,
pulling each other over the road
to grown-up things.
From the side of the truck
out onto the rolling dust and scrub they jump,
tea and bread they've just eaten with the others
a thump in their stomachs when they fall.
Holding hands tight, they jump —
two women in Kosovo leaving behind
their children, their mother, their husbands
gunned down by soldiers
in a roadside café minutes before
and now a mountain of grief
being driven to a mass grave
somewhere these sisters will never find.

One looks back for a second,
feels her whole life piled ugly there,
feels it was beautiful once —
the pull of her man reaching for her
in the middle of the night,
the bitter pain she knew when her four year old
left her for his first day at school,
her mother calling her back home
on a cold winter's night.
Luck chooses where we are born,

passes us through life
unscathed by violence.
Luck is this brave woman now
defying the brutal guards,
rising alive
from her pretend death
and the horror of corpses, the people she's loved —
a frightened survivor pulling
her frightened sister forward,
a sister whispering 'jump!'.

CUTTING HAIR ON NEW YEAR'S DAY

Gulls land on the crumbs of the river
and last year's bicycle gift
is wrapped yellow
in the reflections of the city, its wheels stirring
with each mullet's lazy flip of the Liffey's tail.

Holly wreaths still hang from the hotel's door
and Ormond Quay's sash windows
wink their prickly red-berry eyes
at you and me speeding through the streets,
speeding into the new year

like Flash Kavanagh, loved priest of St Audeon's,
named after his twenty minute mass —
the congregation below in Adam and Eve's
staring up the old hill in envy,
freezing from praying too long.

I have cold fingers, you a cold head.
I'd cut through your hair this morning
and having no newspaper only Christmas wrapping
had sat you down over silver Santas, gold stars,
faceless angels — and clueless, had snipped away.

What do you work at yourself?
Do you want a number one or number two?
Oh how you'd trusted me! Your hair
defiant like feathers, passing through my fingers
blew with us to places we'd always longed to go —

Macchu Pichu, Greenland, The Cooley Pass
and would not let go of us. Even now it clings to us
walking gloveless, hatless through the quiet streets
on New Year's Day, exhaling the old year —
the new one not recognising the clean-cut you.

ON MY FATHER'S BIRTHDAY

I saw silvery ancient lichen
that grows where the air is pure,

deep tap roots of the marram grass
holding the sand-dunes up —

those grasses we painted as children,
put in jam-jars on our windowsills —

a cargo boat crossing the bay,

a dead sea-gull
his legs frozen and green,

the dog whelk shell I blew sand from
and later balanced on my bath edge,

the fluorescent pink dome of the Italian circus tent
far across in Booterstown, its lions roaring like sea,

sky-larks singing spring in,

sand under our nails and grating
the backs of our throats like arguments we've had,

brent geese on mud-flats feeding on eel-grass
far from a Greenland peninsula,

bladderwrack sticking to stone with a substance
scientists want to use for dental glue,

ringed plovers and sanderlings,

oystercatchers with their twitting sounds
more high-pitched than the nervous gulls,

car windows glinting on James Larkin Memorial Road,
his hands a constant memory raised up over O'Connell Street,

terns flying away from Kilbarrack flats
and a top-shell shaped like an emperor's hat,

St Mary Star of the Sea a holy stilt walker,

on the beach the red-coated father carrying one child
on his shoulder, laughing at the others racing the tide,

behind them a Sunday car sinking in the sand,
moss crawling up Mary's hundred feet high stone legs.

And they are us and you long before this day,
calling the sea a name we'd never heard before —

Thalassa, Thalassa, Thalassa,

and we chase after the sliotar
your hurley gives to those holiday waves,

we are young pups walking home with you over rabbits
sleeping deep in the sandy dunes of Cruit island,

we are waiting for fresh fish got
from the currachs at Carrickfinn,

we are waiting for stories to come.

MARLBOROUGH ROAD

On Marlborough Road
the houses have names —
Aclare, Larnaca, Ardeevin,
Shalamar, Woodstock, Hazelhurst
and St Elmo on the way to the station
where the ghost creaked the gate long ago
one early winter morning
and became a wide-eyed Red Setter before me,
as frightened of a girl as I was of him,
our still worlds interrupted.

Going home up Marlborough Road,
I see the garden boats covered in canvas,
the spiked green railings
darker than the hedges
and the copper beech and monkey trees.
The old black Morris Minor is still there
and the domes of the many glass houses.
I hear the shunting of an approaching train
bringing more people home
to this safe, quiet suburb.

And just for this fifteen minute stretch
of house-lined road and hill,
there is peace on Marlborough Road to remember.
I am five years old again, opening our front door,
shocked to see your handkerchief
wave like a flag of blood on your forehead,
and to hear you call my mother's name for help,
your footprints large red accident marks
stronger than the trails left behind you
by birds on our snow-filled drive.

You were my father who growled at nurses — *God almighty,*
how can a child be expected to eat that on her own? —
when, sick in my second year of life, nurses left me
jam sandwiches and a mug of hospital tea.
You were my father who appeared at the top
of Keem Bay, unexpected to us as the thunder storm,
with coats and hats, umbrellas and warm rugs
pulling us safely up the cliff edge and home to holiday beds,
wind and the gulls crying out in joy
Abba, Abba, Abba.

You were our father
my mother watched the kitchen clock for,
climbing up the stairs at five thirty
to make her red lips redder, her bright face brighter
just before we shouted *He's home, he's home!*
leaving behind our laundry-bin lid and kitchen-pot toys
racing each other to open the door to you
and tell of our day's hard work —
of our tree house creations and go-cart inventions,
of the apples and pears we'd stolen from next door's garden.

I have never seen you fall since
but that day your head fell
in tiredness against the train window
just before the flash of Sandymount Strand outside,
then later fell harder onto concrete
halfway along that snowy January road.
And coming home again now, I remember how
you must have slipped, then bled, unfairly vulnerable —
and in my head I want to help you up, brush you clean.
But Marlborough Road's icy beauty keeps pulling my father down.

POEMS FOR BREAKFAST

Another morning shaking us.
The young potted willow
is creased with thirst,
the cat is its purring roots.
Under our chipped window
the frail orange flowers grow.
Now the garden gate clicks.
Now footsteps on the path.
Letters fall like weather reports.
Our dog barks, his collar clinks,
he scrambles, and we follow,
stumble over Catullus, *MacUser*,
Ancient Greek for Beginners,
cold half-finished mugs of tea,
last week's clothes at the bed's edge.
Then the old stairs begin to creak.

And there are the poems for breakfast —
favourites left out on the long glass table.
We take turns to place them there
bent open with the pepper pot,
marmalade jar, a sugar bowl —
the weight of kitchen things.
Secret gifts to wake up with,
rhythms to last the whole day long,
surprises that net the cat, the dog,
these day that we wake together in —
our door forever opening.

AFTER READING A POEM
BY YEHUDA AMICHAI

It is mid- February. Crows peck for slugs
in the hardened soil, the day is frail
as sycamores against the cold sky,
the cold sea beyond — under my window
I see a white cat flutter free like snow,
from the farmer's hungry wire fence.

And on the page, the memory of you
burnt to death in the camps. You were just twenty —
if alive, you'd be old now, a woman nearing eighty —
but once, little Ruth, a child not knowing
they would take you away, stamp you with stars,
cruel insignias of their own hatred of you

and those you loved, those that belonged to you.
Where is your life that might have been?
The poet goes out with his children now,
the children you never met,
gathers mushrooms in the very forest
he remembers planting with you as a child.

I did not know you, but your life
is still on this earth, a cluster of words
shot like last night's meteorite from the burning
memory of your friend into my waiting mind.
We are bundled together, the poem about you
is also about me — this is how love lives on

quietly, unsuspecting that the turn of a page
would reveal so much, even here in a country house,
at the turn of a new century, far from where
you lived, far from where they killed you,
far from where all memory starts.
The season changes. The trees are on fire.

Summer warmth. The cat snoozes
against the heat of the fence's wooden post
and the azure waves are calling us.
We are leaving the dark forest, little Ruth,
wild flowers a tangled hope in our hair,
and on the beach, my footsteps follow yours

happily, way out to the beginning of the skies.

Valentine's Day

Long-billed birds in marshland; at Aughcasla
we pause to feed ponies with dried grass.
It is all silence now, until above us
the hawk's wide wings are a swooping gasp,
a sand-piper shrieks between claws and then
over the night fields fall the funeral bells,
strangers' headlights hurt the sky.

And we reach the cross dug deep into sand
to remember another
killed in the civil war at this beach's edge —
his fellow volunteers frantic,
scrambling over the Conor Pass,
rough nights like gorse piercing their fear
but still they go on, do not forget.

And memory is a fierce glow
speeding through the Valentine sky;
someone just left, those gone way before.
And us, slipping down the high sand dunes,
our recent words inconsequential rain
on our flaming cheeks, our fingers held tight together,
this full world ours to forgive and forget in.

MINT GATHERERS

While you are off gathering mint,
we stain our fingers
with a fresher smell
in the long, narrow room —
its tiny window making
four perfect purple squares
out of the far away mountain —
that room with the yellow blanketed bed
that holds us wrapped in heat and love
over the kitchen, below the Alpine spider,
our own spindly guard and his soft cylindrical web
in the angle of the latticed door.
The house is ours for that brief time

while you are off gathering mint
in your neighbour's field high on the hill.
You raise your hand in the afternoon heat,
rub water across your cheek, can lick already
the green coolness on the roof of your mouth —
while we back there, taste each other.
There are no words. The lizards lie still
in the cool of the old barn. The lime tree shades
the balcony where we rise at last to stand,
now waiting for you to come back,
certain you'll hang from hooks
in the old kitchen ceiling
a bunch of fresh mint leaves to dry,
just below where we had lain.

SNORKELLING WITH YOU

And so, beneath your things I go,
rummaging to find a pencil —
while you are still way out,
a soft seal head, curious-black
on the blue sea —
to say
what it was I saw.
How your legs moved
as though on the moon,
so slowly over under-sea ridges
that little fish came from beyond
to tickle your ankles,
wiggling their life against one
they'd never know.

Then all the day burst its shafts of light
in thin yellow slants through
the tip of the whirling blue.
I heard my breathing funnel its way
towards clots of sand exploding
into balls of fat wars
as I left you behind
and approached
the arc between sea and sky.
And light looked suddenly cut
like hexagonal jigsaw pieces —
and the top of the ocean
holding up bubbles and foam
was like a hammock,
weighed down with heavy things,
tied to the sky's strong branches.

All of this was there,
reminding me
that I was human and would rise again
to see the beach's rock glistening
and on it
the small gold and turquoise bird
I last saw before going below,
still there,
shaking his long beak wisely,
as if to say to me,
Go under again, go under again —
now you have found it, go under,
for there is the magic you need.

ST PATRICK'S DAY

There are moments of happiness —
me putting on Bob Dylan
to surprise you,
. . .*I'd be sad and blue*
if not for you. . .
an oval green bowl made greener
with hard pears piled inside,
the hum of the drying machine,
water rising and falling
as steam from your skin,
the promise of a walk together
out along the damp streets
towards the copper dome of Rathmines,
your mouth smelling of me,
a book *Entanglements* tangled in our sheets,
its words like a crying child
whingeing for our attention.
But our bed is another world,
ignores all calls.
We are listening to our own music
being added to the music below,
feel the floorboards shake.

And rain drips quietly, slowly outside
from the gutter above our window.
I watch it and count
the seconds before each fall,
then push your knees away
from the small of my back
and cross the white painted floor,

raise the blind to let light in,
see clearly the water's rhythm
beat from the moss-dark gable —
and beyond, over chimney-tops
and sleeping roofs, see the mountains
assured in their own life
calling us to get up, to cross streets,
canals and bridges to get to them.
We have slept too long.

MASTER CHEF

In a little while, will you come and cook the chicken —
climb down our stairs under Vermeer's blue-gowned muse,
pass the four glass squares of our green front door and walk
to the kitchen through the white-washed rooms?

Will you leave the things you love — Robert Bly, Francis Ponge,
Wagner's screeching sirens, and come to look at our chicken?
I want you to pepper and lemon it, thyme it with your fingers,
fatten it with butter, press succulent rhymes under its skin

so that it is a roast of rhythms, metaphors and garlic, clever puns,
limes and lyrics, throbbing oven songs between our sky blue presses.
The cat on the yard wall licks its lips, t-shirts on the washing line
are a stirring armless, headless screen protecting your great work.

Oh master cook, oh my fine poet, my much loved chef, even the man
dangling from the shamrock-green crane that swings over Patrick St.
pauses to inhale your culinary odours rising sweeter than the weed
he inhales before jumping to his death, the crowd below well teased.

We push the kitchen window open, poetry rushing into the skies
a plough, a Venus, a firmament of ideas! —
your hair a scribble of lines, your kiss sweet as a haiku on my cheek,
and this chicken startling the darkness into a well fed dawn.

EMPEROR

While others might relax after love,
he is up and about in his boxer shorts,
watering flowers on the balcony —
not caring that it's overlooked
by a hundred city windows opposite.

Back inside, he pads barefoot
their apartment's wooden floors,
blasts Wagner's *Ride of the Valkyries*,
sucks dates, climbs up on a fold-out chair
to check on the highest shelf

Commodus's exact background
in his encyclopaedia,
before the wood beneath his feet
flips back, his toes are caught red sore
and he shouts his pain to the waking walls.

Then he is that ancient emperor —
everybody, everything against him
and hearing the mob's gleeful roars
in the theatre where his anger rules,
he feeds her to the lions.

SHORT LOVE POEMS

1. New Bridge

We move across each other's new landscape
excitedly, find ourselves on a new bridge
on a clear night walking across water
that has never been crossed before,
balance over a part of a river that has never
been looked down into before,
feel our bodies flip back and forwards
among the lazy mullets,
see the city reflected in our eyes.

2. Buzz of a Change

Gradually you are clear to me,
gradually it is easier to see your nose,
the neat half-moon cut of hair around your ear,
your soft skin surprising mine in a darkened room.
But then, how easily you offend without meaning to —
turning from me in the middle of sleep, snoring loudly
as a sequel to our love, while I am left alone imagining
that outside the sun replaces the moon
and that we are waking from fitful dreams
to each other in another place,
the buzz of change vibrant between our ribs.

3. *New Year, New Century*

Steam rising from my skin,
the water dragging the old year with it
down the insistent plug-hole,
you lighting candles in the bathroom
too close to the curtain, too near to my toes,
your elbow and the toothbrush shelf.
This is how the next hundred years began
for me and you — celery and orange soup
still fresh on our breath, Bacall on the television
helping Bogart her ex-lover escape from prison,
you just talking, talking to me —
presents of new books waiting on our bed
and the past parading gifts of oil and skin lotions.

MOUNTAINS OF SNOW

Mountains of snow
on the grass of Corporation Street —
the wired rowan trees' branches
weighed down with white
that quivers, falls
behind the rusting spiked railings,
the washing on the flats' balconies
like stiff bodies hanging in the cold.

I have left you behind
under your own mountain
of sheets, pillow, crumpled blanket,
sleep hardened like ice around your eyes,
dug deep into the corners
of your dry, unmoving lips.
I cannot hope my mouth
will ever moisten yours,
or that my fingers will gently
prize your look open
to my face only —
I cannot hope for a sun
to melt your ways.

NEWS FROM BALBRIGGAN

Three seals make ripples on the sea's surface,
then rise like submarines, the dog fish just below
flip idly now and then — and above, the trawler's smoke
screens the Cooley and Mourne Mountains. Homing pigeons
are let loose on the pier from an old man's bicycle basket,
young boys leap in for a swim from a small boat's edge,
the little blonde girl, afraid of the waves, builds a sand fortress
and in the studio, the painter paints for himself.

In the city, discarded clothes and mis-matched socks
lie in your hallway and you surface like a seal from your sea
of papers to find a pigeon from Ballbriggan on your balcony
with other news from the outside world — how at City Hall
the scaffolding is gone and the walls are high and bright.
When I return, we will stretch up to its windowsills,
peer at the light and the past — and our future
floating with the dust flakes into a world that we will share.

WOMEN ON A TRAIN, POETS IN A ROOM
After reading Louis Mac Neice

Inside, the locked heart
and the lost key.
Outside, the light winking
on the waste of sea.
I clutch the red book
of hard-won rhymes
and am warmed by its beat
that is easily the rhythm
of this late afternoon
over railway tracks sea-ward —
and know I am not alone.
The women wear rings —
which men are theirs? —
their heads bent reading too.
The girl with her pony-tail bobbing,
has her back to mine,
the plant leaves
on her knees rising,
while beyond the misted window
the rocks growl
like sea men coming for us —
but we speed on, each locked
in our own different hearts,
not giving the key away.

Outside, the light winks on a waste of sea
and I step from the station
into my real home
where poets tell their stories —
the Bog of Moods, a woman
jumping to her death from Putney Bridge,

Hildegard of Bingen's cures...
We write in a winter place of late-night milk and toast,
the cracked floor paint sticking to our bare feet like snow,
the old woman next door making ghost sounds
into the early hours — her Glen Miller playing,
her doors eerily opened and shut — but then
our bedroom shakes us awake with morning
and the secrets of the sumac tree.
We step from the station into a familiar place,
feel it is our home —
find that the light in the room is a poem.

LEAVING A CITY BY TRAIN

Always look at the tip of a city
when you leave it by train —
the highest point of pylons,
church spires, roof tops, copper domes.

And look at other things;
the gorse bushes crunched yellow in farewell,
the man on the road waving like a child at the carriages,
his dog strangely still under rowan trees.

Always look at the houses that are not yours
on lanes you cannot name, at the clouds
hanging low over fields you will never
walk through towards a home.

Always look at the city you are leaving
and remember what you have left behind.
In an old place on a landing
your arms opened like a door to me

your mouth said everything and nothing —
became mine and mine yours for so short a time
it seemed to last forever. What did it matter if later
the rain drilled damp holes into our bones

or if the full mean moon
made our secret night so bright like day,
that someone on the stairs turned back to gawk at us,
and became a messenger fresh with news.

What did it matter? That moment
was a magic cloak pulled around us,
an empty taxi sucking us into its warmest self,
racing us away from a drenched back-street lane.

When you leave the city think of all that
and this — how in another place
I would find you again, on another landing perhaps,
loud with the city's late drinking below

and I would open my arms like a door to you,
pull you in, take you
somewhere you least expect —
though you have been there before —

this time, never let you go.

MAY DAY WEDDING

In the garden they decided names —
Jack for a boy, Lou-Lou or Julia otherwise,
discussed the shape of his nose against hers,
the width of their cheeks, the texture of their skin
and what their child's might be.

He pressed his stomach into hers
and thought he felt a heart-beat there,
under her belly knot and the rough scar
of peritonitis that nearly took her
in her first few months.

He wondered about hospital fees,
about moving to a bigger house —
would he be there when the waters broke?
He rubbed her bottom openly
on the restaurant terrace —

guests below, now and then bored
with talk, glancing upwards.
They felt the bride, casual, radiant —
her dress dishevelled with excitement,
pass between the two of them.

They strolled home —
took out Jack Lemmon and Shirley Mc Laine
in Wilder's *Apartment*, to watch later.
He slept and she took off her dress alone,
his handprint still wrinkling its behind.

MINDING HOUSE

We fight fiercely
but soon forget.
Someone left the fire ashes
smouldering in a plastic bin,
did not wash the fork —
cat food mixes
with casserole —
locked us inside and forgot
where the keys were,
fed brittle chicken bones
to a whining dog,
did not think to defrost properly
the turkey pie pastry that now rolls
into a useless damp ball.
Someone cracked underfoot
the rotten balcony wood.

The wind rattling up the hill
is slamming the belligerent
neighbour's car door,
whisking our cries of 'Go away!
Leave us alone!'
up to the cawing gulls.
The sea, our view from morning to night,
is daubed pink, white and blue,
then black as your hair close to mine.
Animals scratch at the door like children
waking us on Christmas morning
in the very early hours.

The storm is a thousand spirits
ripping apart our carefully labelled gifts.
The house groans at our every step —
and then, there is day.

We are tossed fully awake together
like left-overs. We eat chocolate
and stuffing with pork meat
apples and walnuts,
scraps of honeyed ham —
the cat, peering at us
through the banister bars
is ready to leap.
But the letter box claps us awake.
We call to the dog with the idea of a walk,
force the door open, the hill pulling us
upwards, then down to the beach —
the trees howling,
the rough waves beating the island,
the sky a sheet of grey,
our hands held tight.

STUCK INDOORS

Rain all week
and the dog indoors
dry but discontented,
our sofa a ship of cushions,
newspapers, animal sighs —
the slow, dull hours
like crumbs, itchy on our skin.

And we are sailors
tossed this way and that
by winter's temper.
It breaks down doors,
sets house alarms wailing,
drenches passers-by
with the puddles of its fury —

it even bullies the oak
that groans, bends, snaps —
and history crashes,
cracks the pavement,
sends shudders
like a tidal wave
rolling into our home.

Now fear is a barking dog,
a firework erupting
in our city yard,
hissing quickly to an end
like poison —
and our house sinks
further down.

We wait for light,
we wait for calm,
for the white bird
to come back at last
with news of land,
an olive branch
in its trembling beak

when we can
shake ourselves down,
wash ourselves clean,
brush storm pieces
from our tangled hair
and open wide again our doors,
like Noah's outstretched arms.

DREAM

So many doors you close
this irritable September —
upsetting the epicentre
of what I thought was ours,
niggling at that underground point
where voices and hearts
when angered
can dangerously crack the silence.

So many doors you close.
Mosquitoes inflame
the brains of the city,
a hurricane shatters Florida lives,
on my television I see a man's head
hacked from his body in East Timor.
Inside, you spray yourself
against encephalitis, dig down
to cave yourself away from winds
that are frantic to destroy you,
make weapons to fight off murder.

You close your doors from me
and the world
while I wait outside
for so many days
that people begin to notice —
offer me their daughters' hand-me-downs,
warm soup those cold rush hour evenings,
ask who the hell is inside
that keeps me waiting like this?

It's been so long now
since I've seen you, I say,
that I hardly know myself.

I do not bang on the door, yell through
your box, throw stones
at your various windows,
do not phone you on the hour
every hour or write to you every day —
it not being my style.
Instead I'm the fool who waits
and waits, though you've left me
far behind, banging your doors against me,
the light bulbs dangling in each room
as you move from place to place
not thinking there might be one outside
that thinks of you still, remembers you,
wonders just how you're getting on —
your life moving so inward
that from the street, my face turned upwards,
I can hear it suffocate you.

CHRISTMAS EVE DUCK

I thought at first
it was a pig
wounded by pellets —
this plump, pale gift
of yours to me
late on Christmas Eve.

So pale, so plump,
I thought it had been
skinned alive, dragged up
from the dark rivers
of some life
that could be ours

or injured in the twisting
lanes you race down,
away from me.
I move back, hoping
midnight's crazy clanging
will stop this thing being roasted

with such dedication by you,
but you continue on
until there are no other sounds,
only the sizzle of flesh,
the whir of oven interiors,
fervent as your face in thought.

Turning from me,
your back is a door
firmly closing,
your breath
a wild wind blowing me
out onto the dark roof-top

where I hear this new day
wake to the peal of cathedral bells —
Christmas chanting to the river.

GOETHE IN SICILY
March - May 1787

But let's leave the table now
and go to look down into the street.
A criminal is being reprieved
in honour of Holy Week.
Dressed in white-tail coat, white hat,
he is dragged to a mock gallows.
Soon the Viceroy, the clergymen
and nobility will accompany the host
on foot through mud — and all for Santa Rosalia
who has saved this city from plague.

I scribble with a blunt pen
dipped in an artist's sepia.
In the morning, light washes in.
A servant unlatches the shutters.
From the window I watch torrents of rain
gleam the streets for the procession.
A miracle! the people call out.
A slight wind cannot wrap
man and God in dust now
and rubbish is swept far out to the sea.

But let's leave the table again
and go to look down into the street.
A tall man ignoring all eyes on him,
in a freshly curled and powdered wig
collects money for slaves
captured by Barbary pirates.
*You pay gladly for your follies
but expect others to pay for your virtues!*

46

a shopkeeper cries to this Prince of Palagonia,
his villa a self-made place of horrors

where pedestals carry groups
of hunchbacks, deformed animals —
and every kind of monster emerges
from the bellies of vases.
I will leave his ugliness behind,
and walk in the public gardens of Palermo
under orange and lemon trees heavy with fruit,
the mulberry trees in their freshest greens —
and near oleander and hyacinths
will admire bushes unknown to me.

50 Degrees Celsius

Rubber tyres thrown
from a burning shop —
fire engines blocking the streets.
Overhead, helicopters spray
a limited, frantic rain.
Children cling to parents and cry.
At the bottom of the road
the mountain groans.
The women in the red-curtained hall
fan themselves and say nothing.
The girl sitting at a creaky piano
plays the Warsaw Concerto.
The mayor talks only of money.
We eat green beans, round bread with oil.
But the smoke whirls from houses
below our hot garden and close by
the guards are cutting the gas lines off.

And in the sea the poet drowns,
his skin cooling the hot lava stones
and on the flaming terrace
ants fight in the billow of sheets.
Etna fumes in the distance.
Lovers kiss in the garage,
the hair at the nape of his neck
wiry between her fingers tugging.
No bed for them both here —
his wife and child asleep upstairs.
And the black snake slithers
through the dried grass.
Ants are a bundle
of dismembered parts now.

Tomorrow, we will pass through farm gates
with no farmers to be seen —
only jays fanning the heat with their wings.
But for now, we quietly dress,
search for tickets, money, passports,
before pushing the door open to the heat
that has arrived in our very home.
And there seems nowhere to go.

HEART ATTACK

Was it over the dry hills
of Sardinia
or closer to Milan
that my heart chose to swing
north of my body,
draining me of all colour
and laid me flat, floating
under air hostesses
and a doctor on holiday
gaping concern?

While you all landed
emergency style in Rome,
and paramedics heaved me
onto a bright orange
canvas stretcher,
you didn't notice
how its steel handles
were as cold as my skin now,
or that I was gone over the ocean
to Palermo and further

glad to be free of it all —
joyous to find Christ
fallen in a Cefalu sacristy,
raising him up
to the mosaic apostles
and winged messengers of hope,
my soul newly placed
in the siesta heat, the sun
through the arched windows
my certainty.

POEM

I have found you again
like once in Bagheria
when we lay awake at night
pretending to be asleep
in the sticky July heat,
then woke the others
testing Sicilian tarot cards —
hand of cups
empress
emperor
what will be our lives...?

I have found you again
not in the Villa of Pallagonia —
the deformed monsters,
the gothic serpents sneering,
the ballroom's mirrored dome
fogged over by the cracked centuries,
the endless decisions
and late night calls
waiting for her to arrive —
instead I have found you
in this poem you wrote
that suddenly splits
my Saturday toast
with clarity.

I see the words opening
high as your old flat's ceiling,
see you touch her hand
across the chipped red-painted table,

boil the old kettle for two,
see you drink alone,
sleep in your room
she in her's —
the sparrows scattering twigs
down the numerous chimneys
like mice sounds at night
answering your silence with a noise.

Then your lines on this page to read.

PAINTER AT WORK
for Clement Mc Aleer

You have been painting all night.
A sea has rushed through your head,
dragged you way down under an idea
that must roll its way into your evening.
You have felt it would come all day —
your eyes glazing over when others spoke,
your distracted reach for a brush
you picked up, then put down,
the time not right, just yet.

In your flat, your door is firmly closed
and the light under your door is sharp, says go away!
People come and go. The meat is roasted and eaten.
Cigarette smoke asks after you.
In your absence we play your music,
find in your notebooks ideas you sketched,
hear through the wall nothing,
though your open-laced shoes flung on the floor,
your jacket slouched on the door knob
tell us that you're still here.

The ending is always quiet.
A picture fills a space, then is with you everywhere —
balances over the kitchen work-top where you scoop
muesli into your dazed morning mouth, is hung
just above bath water where you soak for ages
unsettles the dust you forgot was thick on your bedside table,
is pinned high in the sky over streets you walk down
to your studio, your city becoming its rhythm
until at last you are satisfied.

You come home and this painting is a gift —
a bright sea view when someone is feeling low,
a vast landscape to arrive at when others gave up hope.
The hard work over, you can talk
freely of your day now,
mix olives with feta cheese and greens,
raise your glass, your lips,
your eyes, your heart,
to the life that will be painted again.

At Work

Isn't it better that you work
in your room
and I in mine, meeting only
for late night korma, pizzas, noodles
paid for with whatever we can find
at the back of sofas, on windowsills,
at the bottom of our vases and jugs
circled with the left-over green
of flowers long since dead?

Isn't it better we work
this way — alone, until we meet
not saying how differently we make
sense out of the air, fighting
our separate devils that enter
without a key. Ruthless, drunken,
aggressive past, lies, ex-lovers,
childhood fears, tangled secrets unspoken,
all written forever in both our rooms?

We meet bleary-eyed, silent —
each knowing the other well.

DIARY OF A FAT MAN

I am so fat now
that the woman I love
will not lie down with me —
so I make her shape in the mountains
of potatoes I boil and mash,
feel her breasts in the dough I knead and prick,
her bread nipples rising erect at 200 degrees Celsius,
hear her noises gurgling with the bubbling
of tomato, ginger, cinnamon,
her kisses extra sweetness oozing.

Skin, heaped spoons of crème fraîche,
eyes, sharp kiwi green,
arms, the curve of bananas, melons, fresh bread rolls,
mouth, a dazzling lemon split apart —
I am so fat now
she is all of this to me and more.
I make my bed in the sitting room,
unable to climb the stairs.
I sleep with my heavy boots on,
unable to pull them off.
Sometimes she passes by my door —
the dart of a thin shadow,
her breasts suddenly shrivelled
as an avocado's outer layer,
her skin rough like uncooked rice,
her eyes two empty plates pleading,
I look at you
and can never eat again.

Her voice has the rancid stench
of food left over for weeks.
She is becoming nothing —
ice-cream melted on a hot kitchen floor,
boiled water evaporating in a room.
But I make her again — my woman.
Her love among the carrots, onions,
broccoli, steak and garlic
is so heated in my thick, tasty stew
that I do not notice
her open the front door
then leave the house for good —
the smell of food
a jaded world forever clinging
to her hair, her skin and clothes.
Not hearing, I scoop, scoop,
scoop from my pot
into the biggest
bowl I can find.

ANNAGHMAKERRIG

1. Deer

A deer met me on a lane
I didn't know —
so far ahead at the blur of ditches
and the forest slopes
that I thought at first it was a tall man
his antler height like thin arms
stretched overhead waving,
or an elegant figure suddenly stepping out,
making itself real
from an oil painting.

Both of us turned away,
afraid to stir the other's quiet.
There was only a mud way, its middle
heaped with stones between us,
only a bird more intent
on its own life warblings
half listening to our moves,
only the dull buzz of a fly agitating our silence —
and yet we felt the whole world
had stopped to watch us.

We turned away, then back again,
each fascinated by either being there,
flanked by the towering humility of trees —
the wind speeding like cars
through the highway of branches,
your ribs and mine heaving a place
in the rustling copper and silver month
we had found ourselves in.

And I understood you knew ways
I had not yet found —

envied your cool turning
into the mass of dark greens
tangling upwards to the sky,
each soft step of yours such a gentle tremor
that leaves fell in quiet reassurance,
guiding your uphill path.
If I followed, your eyes would be a light for me,
your body a blanket in the thicket of fear.
If I followed, I knew there would be
no reason to ever go back.

2. Ghost

This is the ghost that makes it clear,
the ghost that flaps open doors
in the wood-ceilinged study,
making people from old photographs
come to life and walk again through the house
that was theirs hundreds of years ago.
This is the ghost that breathes in the dining-room,
as we lounge on sofas and the window seat,
after Sunday lunch, after organic wine,
after the salad that will be loved forever.

The voice of the poet is wise,
floats to our ears from the tape machine,
stirs our silences, our inner sadness,
our loneliness, our need for love,

saves us from all that stops us being ourselves.
And this is the ghost of change,
of all things possible,
of your eyes closed, listening to the poem,
your nose turned to the garden,
its weeds and daffodils, its water tower.

This is the ghost of questions not spoken
but answered between us with no words,
so that when at last we climb to the attic room
or the wide desk that looks to the lake
we think how we'll soon walk assured
down the forest-lined road alone,
how we'll soon be at one with the deer,
the oncoming tractor, the endless weather —
think that this ghost keeps on howling
through our hearts but we will not be afraid.

WALKING WITH AN ARCHITECT
for Ray Mc Ginley

I see things differently
when walking with you —
the footbridge over a part of the Liffey
we've never crossed before
that should have your roof design
with petal-shaped sails to keep
other walkers dry from our grey city rain,
the beauty of the old bank's edifice
kept so well we spend ages
just chatting about it by a bus stop
near Trinity College,
while the old woman with her trolley
listens, looks up and thinks of things
that never bothered her before, like
mullions, columns, pediments, pilasters.

This city is ours
to look at, inspect,
full of concrete, wood and plaster —
the thoughts of men on paper
belonging to years ago that became
sketches of shadows and light,
the gasp of astonishment
we still see on our way
to work and home.
While in cars, on buses,
scooters and bicycles,
only the odd person
now and then notices
what to them
has just always been there.

I see things differently
when walking with you,
when we play
our favourite city game —
we pass cathedrals, shops,
office blocks, banks,
until we stop at one tall oak door
standing as wide and high
as six twenty foot men
side by side on Werburgh Street.
And with our fingers we press
the wooden smoothness of its shape
only to find it secretly open —
left carelessly so
this Friday's rush hour.

And we were suddenly inside
in the darkness
with no alarm bells ringing,
no stranger's hand
on our shoulders,
no security men
asking why.
Whether we should
move up the stairs
or out again into the noisy night,
we don't know.
Wondering which way to go,
we say nothing
move nowhere —
love the stillness of it all.

Somebody Has Died Close By

Somebody has died close by
in an old part of the city,
on a lane at the side of our flat —
a lane that I trudge up
every day and evening,
not noticing much.
But today somehow, the light
on the Castle windows made me look up
and I saw flowers on a drain-pipe
with notes flapping like leaves
We'll miss you, or *May your soul soar* —
and then, *Rest in Peace*.

While you and I were sipping
late-night whiskey, banging doors
against each other's words,
or were just knotted together,
quiet in our dark sleep worlds,
somebody had died close by.
And thinking this, I felt
City Hall's windows rise
out of their gleaming walls,
their light shaped like a ghostly procession
of people I never knew,
who had trudged up this lane before.
Then from the cupped hands of that moment,
gulls, like a spray of white spirit crumbs,
flung themselves far out across the sky
that had seemed small to me —
but was suddenly vast, unending.